ELLE DECOR
PORTFOLIOS

PATIOS AND VERANDAS

Cover: photo © Guillaume de Laubier
Reportage Marie-Claire Blanckaert

Copyright © 2003 Filipacchi Publishing for the present edition
Copyright © 2003 Editions Filipacchi, Société SONODIP – *Elle Décoration*, for the French edition

Translated from French by Fern Malkine-Falvey
Copyedited by Matthew J.X. Malady

ISBN: 2 85018 654 6

Color separation: Hafiba
Printed and bound in France by Clerc

PATIOS AND VERANDAS

filipacchi
publishing

The main function of patios, covered courtyards and verandas, is to extend the inside of the house to the outdoors, or to bring nature into the house itself. In the past, only those who lived in warm climates could experience the luxury of patios; now they are found everywhere. To design beautiful patio settings, landscapists and decorators utilize all their ingenuity in order to create miniature gardens often accompanied by teak furniture, terra cotta pots and planters teeming with flowers and other aromatic plants.

Out in the countryside, covered courtyards transform outdoor patios into dining rooms and summertime living rooms. Greenhouses become multi-purpose rooms unto themselves.

Journalists from *Elle Decor* have traveled the world to bring you pictures that will not only make you aware of the dreams of others, but that will be of help to you as you attempt to realize your own designing dreams.

CONTENTS

TERRACES

IN LANDS WHERE THE SUN IS KING, SOUND PLANNING FOR THE USE OF VERDANT AREAS IS A NECESSITY. NO MATTER WHAT THE SEASON, A TERRACE—WHETHER IN THE COUNTRYSIDE OR BY THE SEA—PROVIDES A MARVELOUS PLACE TO GARDEN, RELAX OR RECEIVE GUESTS.

Left. This terrace floor features a far wall and furniture made of teak. Bamboo and ivy grow in flower boxes behind the wall. On the left, columns of ivy surround the bench. Box hedges, cypress, palm and olive trees grow in large flowerpots. The umbrella is Chinese.

Above. Landscapist Pierre Alexandre Risser has surrounded this teak bench with trimmed hedges, rose bushes and imitation jasmine. On the left is a magnolia tree pruned in the shape of a pyramid. In the foreground, Butterfly lavender and rosemary.

Left. Architect Laurent Bourgois has completely transformed this lovely, rectangular terrace in the heart of Paris. To give it more intimacy, he has covered the metal fence with a double trellis, and in the middle has placed earthen pots full of plants.

Right. Since the terrace connects the living room to the bedroom, a portico of iroko wood was installed to separate the two sections in a graceful manner. Jasmine and wisteria cover the portico which transforms the space into two distinct rooms of greenery. Plants and shrubs overflow from earthenware tubs decorated in iroko shingles. The flooring is made of stone slabs from Bourgogne.

Left. At Jacqueline Hagnauer's house, French windows from the living room open out onto the terrace, and help to extend those long summer days. Jacqueline has used a red and white color scheme. The red comes from her rhododendrons and climbing roses, the white, from anthemis, arum lilies and iberis. Since many of the plants—such as the box hedges, camellias and thujas—keep their leaves year 'round, she is surrounded by vegetation all year long.

Right. Laurence and Philippe Brunon's terrace is so large that landscapist Olivier Riols has planted a small herb garden on it. Parsley, chives, chervil and mint are separated at regular intervals by small hedges. The slatted floor is made of teak, and the chairs are draped in raw linen slipcovers.

TERRACES

Below. In Paris, an outstanding gardener has transformed her rooftop into a vegetable garden, mixing bulbs with roses, hydrangeas, strawberries, fennel, angelica and other aromatic herbs.

Right. In Milan, one dines on this charming terrace amidst the blooming roses and fruit trees— all of which lend a romantic air to the city.

Above. On this terrace redesigned by landscapist Laurent Bourgois, Louis Benech has mixed honeysuckle, jasmine and variegated ivy along the lattice fencing at the edge of the balcony. Pittosporum and viburnum reside in the flowerpots throughout.

Right. The rear of the late Gianni Versace's house opens onto a garden patio enclosed by trellises and enlivened by a bubbling fountain. The result is an oasis of vegetation in the middle of Manhattan.

Above. Clutter and lack of organization are common prior to the redecoration of a terrace. **Right.** Why not make a change for the better? Only a few items were needed here. The terrace was redesigned using an ewer, a watering can, vases, small buckets, and a basin—all of which are made of galvanized steel. Several earthen pots and saucers, gloves, a gardening fork, some boxes of seedlings, plastic clogs, a metal patio heater, a metal plate warmer, folding chairs and an aluminum pedestal table add the final touches. In a short period of time, your terrace, like this one, can be transformed into a professional site.

In the foreground of
this terrace is a flower
box made of braided
wicker and lined with
treated felt. A slatted,
wooden flooring,
ceramic platters,
outdoor pillows,
folding wooden tables,
goblets made of blown
glass, a glass pitcher,
and glass lanterns
with black lacquered
metal trim are
all incorporated
to transform the
previously barren space
into a salon worthy
of receiving guests.

Left. Here we see a perfect example of a terrace that has been transformed into a dining room. The armchairs are by Lloyd Loom and the table base is cast iron; eating utensils are stainless steel with boxwood handles; and the earthenware dishes are by d'Astier de Vilatte. The lanterns are suspended from painted metal supports. The flowerpot with its matching saucer is made of clay, and the bistro table is of recycled zinc.

Below. Laurence and Philippe Brunon have transformed this balcony into a summer lounge. The deck chairs are in teak. Along the back trellis, three strategically placed cordyline indivisas in their teak planters create an exotic atmosphere.

Left. Publicist Fabienne Boudet has made this terrace her office. She is surrounded by rose-colored Mrs. Meilland roses, white Iceberg roses, and deep red President L. Senghor roses—all mixed together amidst a confusion of rhododendrons and irises.

Right. Here is a corner where one can relax in the shade. The rattan sofa and armchairs are by Claudia. In front of them is a teak folding table. On the table, a rattan tray is brimming with glasses of orangeade and an ice bucket. Pillows made of kilim have been placed on the sofa for two. Initially, the floor consisted of dreadful-looking gravel. It is now a beautiful slatted floor. Surrounding the terrace, a gorgeous green trellis is adorned with climbing white roses.

Left. All that was needed to transform this excessively long and narrow balcony were some meticulously chosen decorations and a carefully selected mixture of colored plants. This passageway has now become a cozy area where one can rest and meditate undisturbed, far from the gaze of others.
Below. This balcony has been turned into a beautiful terrace as a result of the careful management of every square inch of its surface. A white tarpaulin has been attached to an arbor constructed to create shade. A cluster of clematis armandii and climbing Iceberg roses grow along the railing. In the planters, laurel trees, hellebores and box hedges.

Left. Antiques dealer Gordon Watson's terrace in London has a covered floor, giving the impression that the apartment is extended to the outdoors. An English-style bench from the 1920s stands in sharp contrast to the lacquered garden furniture. The cluster of plants, along with the turn-of-the-century Moroccan kilims, makes the terrace look both comfortable and exotic.

Above. Nicole Mugler's apartment in Paris opens onto a terrace where, in the spring, sparrows sing joyfully in the shade of the bamboo and climbing rose bushes. The table is set for breakfast in the sunshine. The porcelain tea set from Sèvres dates back to the 1850s, and the jelly pot is from the 18th century. For the flooring, a kilim rug.

Above, left. When this patio was redecorated. the original zinc floor was preserved.

Above, right. In this terrace in the Vendée region of France, the wisteria. laurel and wild clematis exude a wondrous fragrance.

Right page. For this cozy urban terrace. the goal was to create the atmosphere of a sunlit veranda. This effect was successfully achieved by installing white, diamond-shaped trellises against walls painted yellow.

TERRACES

Below. Alain-Dominique Perrin, executive director of Richemont, installed this terrace in front of his château in Lagrezette, near Cahors. The floor consists of large slabs of stones from the region. The terrace is shaded by an arbor. On the bare, wooden table surrounded by benches and armchairs, he enjoys meals with friends and family.

Right. The bed installed in this salon-style corner of a terrace in Neuilly was found at a flea market. The owner has arranged a variety of pillows on the bed, and has placed pedestal tables on a floor covered with straw matting. On the right, mixed in with the bamboo, are a rose-colored Sharifa Asma rose and a long-stemmed Iceberg rose.

Left. The teak flooring on Patrick Frèche's terrace can be dismantled. **Below.** The terrace of this triplex apartment, near the Bois de Boulogne in Paris, exudes a feeling of strength, moderation and serenity.

Above. Kevin Baker has converted the rooftop of this small, three-story building in Seattle into a terrace. Although the maple trees aren't in bloom yet, large earthen pots filled with flowering white cyclamens remind us that spring is near.

Above. In the backyard of an apartment
on the Upper East Side in New York City, we
come upon this verdant patio. Two bamboo
"curtains" define the space and seem to
draw us into the summer dining room. The
pair of forged iron lanterns are Moroccan.

Left. Decorator Anne-Marie de Ganay had two stone benches made for the terrace of this country dwelling. Once a convent, it is now a private home. In the summertime, she places white cushions on the benches. In the evening, one can have a drink, watching the sun set on the Petit Luberon mountain range.

Below. Michelle Joubert has worked wonders with this château in Gignac. It was never finished, and had not been lived in since the 18th century. Terraces and ponds liven up the exterior of this family dwelling in the Vaucluse region. From one of the terraces, we have this view of the Luberon Mountains.

TERRACES

Below. Tony Facella's Moorish-style home is situated between the sea and the medina of Hammamet. Its vast garden is arranged in layers of terraces that partially disappear amidst the vegetation. The summertime living room is comfortably furnished with Tunisian-style, sculptured wooden sofas and armchairs.

Right. "When designing a room, I consider the number of people that it will be able to seat," says Valentino, the famous couturier. "Discomfort, along with pretentiousness, is the worst error in taste that one can commit when decorating." Valentino obviously applied this philosophy when designing this terrace.

Above. In Tangier, nothing is obvious.
But marvels like this terrace built off a
house in the Casbah await us at every turn.

Above. In the Rothschild's home north of the island of Corfu, the terrace, bordered by a stone bench, offers a view of the port of Kouloura.

TERRACES

Above. At painter Teddy Millington-Drake's house on the island of Patmos, copper lanterns illuminate a terrace overlooking the sea. The imposing, whitewashed, inclined walls serve as back support for the cushions, creating an unusual resting area.

Above. By remaining true to local traditions as he restored this 17th-century house, Teddy was able to adapt it perfectly to the harsh climate of the region. In order to get through the hot summer nights, he designed an ottoman, covered it in ticking, and placed it on a raised platform.

This divan, on the second floor of Teddy
Millington-Drake's home in Greece, is
covered in upholstery linen ticking. It invites
us to take a siesta in the great outdoors.

Above. At Millington-Drake's once again, the large stone table on one of the many terraces that adorn this house, is set for lunch in the open air.

Right. The property has several terra that are covered with arbors. This on is draped in bougainvillea, which hel shelter the terrace from the hot sun.

Above. Meals are served on one of two terraces, depending on the host's mood. The "Malcontenta" chairs that encircle the stone pedestal table are originals. They were designed by English decorator John Stefanidis, and are based on a neoclassic design.

Above. This comfortable, white-walled, subdivided terrace is full of nooks and crannies. Here, "everything is done in order to make even the most difficult guest feel immediately comfortable, as if they were in their own home," says Millington-Drake.

Left. The owner of this house in South Corsica designed the sofas, with cushions covered in linen, for this terrace/salon. They were constructed by Gérard Amsallem.
Above. On days when the heat is too much to take, one can find protection from the sun on this sheltered terrace with teak flooring.

Above. During the summer in Cavallo, an island south of Corsica, large, comfortable rattan sofas are placed on the outdoor terrace of this stone house decorated by Giovanna Rainieri.

TERRACES

Architect Bogdan Brzeczkowski conceived of the idea to build this house in the middle of five acres of impenetrable brush in the south of Corsica. The owners then decided to remove enough of the undergrowth to expose the boulders underneath, which now surround the house. The house was purposely constructed to face due west, thereby allowing for a full view of the sunset. Here, among the boulders, the dining room has been set for dinner.

Right. Famous hairdresser John Frieda's house in Connecticut was designed to offer a yearlong view of the lake and mountains as the seasons change. On the terrace that links the living room to the bedroom, he has installed a desk he found at a flea market in New York. The panoramic view allows one to observe the fauna and flora on the far side of the lake.

Below. On the edge of Candlewood Lake, breakfast at Frieda's is served in this perfectly enchanting setting. The terrace consists of a pontoon that has been converted to allow for gatherings.
Right page. Below the house, a table and chairs made of weathered teak welcome guests to a summer meal.

Left. High above Cape Town in South Africa, this terrace was designed specifically so that one could take full advantage of the seemingly endless swimming pool.

Above. From the front of this house, one has an impressive view of the Bantry Bay—seen here under a brilliant sky. Cleverly designed wooden shutters shield the sun.

Above. This terrace, with its whitewashed walls, suspended over the Turkish port of Bodrum, awaits its guests for their apéritif.

Right. A terrace encircles the entire top floor of this apartment in Paris. The floors here are made of iroko wood.

GREENHOUSES AND PATIOS

WHETHER ANNEXED TO A HOUSE OR INSTALLED AT THE END OF THE GARDEN, GREENHOUSES AND PATIOS CAN BE TRANSFORMED INTO DINING ROOMS, LIVING ROOMS OR PEACEFUL HAVENS. ALL ONE NEEDS IS A LITTLE IMAGINATION.

Left. This slightly raised winter garden utilizes a corner of the house where the family likes to gather and have its meals.

Above. This greenhouse/patio is bathed in light, yet sheltered from intemperate weather. It has become a full-time living room.

Left and above. In Dominique Kieffer's enclosed patio/dining room, the gardener's table—which is usually covered with a variety of pots—is on occasion transformed into a festive dining room table. On the wrought iron bed in the background, there are a variety of pillows covered in fabrics from a collection by Kieffer. The floor is covered in sea grass.

Left. In this gorgeous winter garden, antiques dealer Alain Demachy displays a breakfast setting by Sèvres on a green patina wrought iron table. Four 19th-century armchairs, decorated in swirling grapes and vines, encircle the table. The cast-iron fireplace, with its brass pipe, is made by Sauvaire. In the background, behind the footstool by Gaudí, two armchairs made of steel come from a military campaign of the 18th century. The French, painted ceiling of sheet metal is from the time of Napoleon and the needlepoint rug is from the era of Napoleon III.

Right. A green, diamond-shaped trellis enhances the already grand interior of this winter garden.

GREENHOUSES AND PATIOS

Muriel Brandolini, the famous New York
decorator, has transformed the patio at
her home in the Hamptons into a dining
room/winter garden. The dim light
filtering through the straw venetian
blinds, the Tunisian rug, and the chairs
by Marc Newson all seem to conspire
to create a warm and cozy atmosphere.
She has added a table by Jansen,
an Egyptian-style upholstered settee
and imitation-bamboo chairs.

Above. In Pierre Bergé's garden in Paris, we find this patio. It is an island of greenery, with its Proustian-like charm and seclusion. The tableware is set on a table by Poillerat. On the left, a console designed by Louis Cane. The wrought iron chairs date back to the 1950s.

Above. For his office/patio, Bergé asked
François-Josef Graf to design a structure
that would allow him a splendid view of the
garden. When Paris awakens, six Australian
parakeets launch into song, and the light
from the small lamps softly fades.

Left. For Anouska Hempel's winter garden—which is based on one built in the 19th century—a large, metal archway with curved glass predominates.

Above. This suspended garden, with its glassed-in living room, is in Frederico de Freitas' house/museum in Madeira. The residence was referred to in the 19th century as "the house of pleasures."

VERANDAS AND COVERED COURTYARDS

NEITHER COMPLETELY OUTSIDE NOR INSIDE, A COVERED COURTYARD SHIELDS ONE FROM THE HEAT, THE RAIN AND THE WIND. IT EXTENDS THE LENGTH OF THE HOUSE, AND ALLOWS A VIEW OF THE GARDEN. THE VERANDA IS AN ADDED BONUS—AN EXTRA SPACE WHERE ONE CAN RELAX AND RECEIVE GUESTS IN THE MOST PLEASANT SURROUNDINGS.

Left. In Yves Saint Laurent's home in Marrakech, the colors used for the veranda harmonize with the fountain, which is bordered by bamboo, coconut trees and oleander.

Above. The sheltered courtyard at Pierre Bergé's house borders a garden redesigned by Pascal Cribier. The armchairs were bought at Alexandre Biaggi's antiques store.

Left. At the Tahitian home of architect Pierre Lacombe, a pavilion has been erected at the far end of the swimming pool. There, in the shade of a wooden-tiled roof, his friends and family can enjoy a drink. The outdoor furniture is Indonesian, Indian and Polynesian. The pool overflows its walls. It is lined with slabs of green stone that blend in perfectly with the environment.

Right. This swimming pool in Bangkok is at the center of four traditional-styled pavilions. The roofs are typical of those built in Chieng Mai. Near the sofas, an earthen jar from the 19th century overflows with orchids.

Left. At this house in
Tahiti, meals are served
on the veranda, where
one is protected from
the sun's heat.

Right. This living
room sits on the edge
of a waterfall-like
swimming pool.
The border of the pool
is a pale yellow,
which matches the
color of the beach.
The flooring is terrazzo,
and the furniture is
Indonesian in design.

VERANDAS AND
COVERED COURTYARDS

Above. In this open-air living room of the Amanpuri Hotel on an island in the Indian Ocean, sunlight reflects off the wood and the palm trees. The use of space, the shade and the flowers add to the serenity of the setting, inviting us to lose ourselves in relaxation.

Above. The design used for the railings of this veranda in Corsica mirrors that often used for railings in the Bahamas and the French Caribbean. The cushions adorning the rattan sofas are covered in white linen.

The hammock comes from a trip to Brazil. Guy André, Guy Breton, Boguslaw Brzeczkowski and Jean-Marc Roques, four architects of the GEA (Groupement d'études architecturales), conceived this house.

Left. Beneath the roof of this house in Corfu, a veranda/living room awaits its guests for those warm summer nights.

Above. To prolong the enchantment, breakfasts are served on this veranda teeming with jasmine and wisteria.

VERANDAS AND
COVERED COURTYARDS

Above. Not far from Marseilles, buried deep
in the heart of a pine forest in Provence, we
come upon the Pastré family's dwelling. When
the Countess de Pastré lived here long ago, she
used this covered courtyard, with its high
vaulted ceilings, as her summer dining room.

Above. In the 17th century, the Count de
Grivel wanted to share the beauty of his
property on Mauritius island with as many
people as possible. Soirees, cocktail parties
and private receptions were held beneath this
covered courtyard/summertime living room.

Left; above, bottom. On the islet of Moyo in Indonesia, this open-air bungalow/dining room of the Amanwana hotel is situated right next to a nature preserve facing the sea. The sofas are arranged in a comfortable fashion.

Above, top. This luxurious veranda facing the Java Sea—where tortoises, whales and dolphins commonly frolic—has been transformed into a bungalow where guests are received.

VERANDAS AND
COVERED COURTYARDS

Above. In Tunisia, sturdy pillars supporting graceful archways create a luxurious veranda in the front of this house. The owners are delighted by the effect that whitewashed walls have with the white rattan furniture.

Above. In Hammamet, we find a closed universe created by Violett and Jean Henson in the 1930s. Beneath the vaulted ceiling, belladonna lilies and banana saplings reside. The mosaic floor is Roman in style. The colonnades are made of whitewashed sandstone.

Left. For Tony Facella, the goal was to incorporate the landscape into his house. He successfully achieved this by blending a tree trunk into the middle of his white, summertime living room.

Right. The veranda at the Cotton House hotel faces a terrace situated directly on the white sand of Mustique. As a result, one can prolong the beneficial effects of swimming in the crystal clear waters off of this Caribbean island.

Left. At designer Valentino's house in Rome. we see beige rattan furniture and a white monochromatic theme around the pool. The tent was inspired by a similar one found at the Royal Pavilion in Brighton.

Above. In a garden at twilight, a waterproof. double-layered tent-top with drawstring curtains in striped Dralon creates an attractive, theatrical-like setting for dinner under a chandelier.

Left. In this veranda in Corsica, we find teak weathered by the elements. Sofas and armchairs, designed by Julie Prisca, are covered in raw linen. The wall lights made of driftwood were created by the owner of the house.

Right. The top of this table in the outdoor dining room is made of 4-inch-thick lava. The table has been strategically placed on the side of the house that faces the sea.

Left. At Marie-José Pommereau's, the tabletop is made of shale, and is perched on a base of red cedar. The table is set with earthenware plates. The bench cushions are covered in a striped fabric. The armchairs are made of teak.

Right. A dining room was installed by decorator Giovanna Rainieri on this veranda to take advantage of the summer months. It features a cleverly designed pulley system that allows one to gracefully raise the surrounding walls.

Left. On the Brazilian coast, where sand, sea, sun and wind meet, a huge parasol-like roof shelters the family from the elements. This outdoor living space makes use of rattan and braided rope furniture from Bahia. The vase is sintered glass.

Right. One of Paris' most famous antiques dealers, Jean-Michel Beurdeley, lives in Bangkok. At his home, a traditional lacquered, wooden gazelle greets the owners at the entranceway of their outdoor living room.

Left. In Moka, on the island of Mauritius, we find "Eureka," the museum/home that once housed the Le Clezio family. Here we see a luxuriously arranged table, set in peaceful surroundings. The young owners were passionate about redesigning the garden on "Bel-Air," their private estate.

Right. In order to escape the "grays" and emphasize the "blues," this veranda in Cargese, Corsica, faces the sea. Chairs and armchairs are made of wrought iron, and the cushions are covered in raw linen. The 1940s table is made of wood and tinplate.

Left. Philippe Starck's house is located in the middle of a clearing on a property near Paris. Birch trees and rhododendrons surround the house, which is made of wood and glass. One dines on a veranda simply lit by ceiling lights with white lampshades. The owner created the table and chairs.

Right. This veranda is overflowing with charm. A good old sofa was placed here for the occasion. It is surrounded by a rocking chair, and chairs found at a flea market. Add an Adirondack chair hanging from the ceiling, made of ash wood from a kayak, and the setting is picture perfect.

Here in a lovely corner of Antwerp.
Belgium. one can sit and have a cup of
coffee in the shade of a large tarpaulin
parasol. Potted hedges surround the aged.
rattan furniture. The bricks have been
arranged in a chevron pattern.
During the summer, the French windows
that open onto the living room are left open.

Above. Through an aperture in the veranda wall. we can observe the interconnecting gardens of a home near Paris. An imitation. espalier-shaped pear tree made of sheet metal adorns the inside wall.

Right. In this house in Italy. beneath an arbor constructed of braided bamboo and a linen awning. we find bamboo armchairs with back and seat cushion slipcovers made of cotton canvas.

VERANDAS AND
COVERED COURTYARDS

Below. When the weather is pleasant at this country house near Paris, breakfast and dinner are served on the veranda. Garden baskets are hung from the rafters, while a chest in the background is buried in begonias.

Right. On this veranda, the stone benches are decorated with mattresses and seat cushions covered in raw linen. The tables are made of iroko wood—which is less expensive than teak, yet endowed with the same properties. The lamps are Indian urns with metal shades.

Above. At Yves Taralon's home, this covered courtyard at the far end of the garden is ideal for resting. To emphasize the rustic atmosphere, the decorator has installed some furniture made of logs. On the bed, sheets by Porthault, from a design by Olivier Gagnère.

Right. This tiled roof was added to the side of the Hôtel Chaufourg in the 19th century. Although the back area was originally closed off to protect against the mistral winds, it was later reopened so that one can view the fig tree and vines.

Left. The table in this
Provençal home is laid
out beneath chestnut
beams. One end of
the beams rests on
the branches of a
100-year-old tree.
At night, one can dine
by lantern light.

Right. In the evening,
meals are served under
this pergola built on
the remains of a
cloister in Luberon.
It is surrounded by
begonias, honeysuckle,
jasmine and wisteria.

Left. At first glance, Tangier is not a pretty city. But plunge into the maze of streets— where you can discover a patio sheltered by the shade of a fig tree— and you understand why writers, artists and travelers have always been fascinated by this place.

Right. In the Henson's house in Hammamet, a Roman cornice serves as a bench on one of the terraces on the property.

Left. This one-story house in Corsica faces both the sea, and a grove of palm and olive trees. Easy chairs await the owners under the pergola covered with bougainvillea.

Right. During long summer days, this sheltered courtyard of a house in the Cévennes region of France is perfect for enjoying the view of the plains of Languedoc.

Left. A cascade of greenery can always be found in the winter garden of Anouska Hempel's English manor. The garden furniture is made of rattan, and the pillow slipcovers are made of striped linen cloth.

Above. In Funchal, in Madeira, the winter garden in Frederico de Freitas' home/museum is in the Thonet style. Teeming with ferns, the stone and concrete floor is typical of the region.

VERANDAS AND
COVERED COURTYARDS

Below. In Pierre Bergé's home, this veranda serves to extend the summer dining room area. Architect Didier Boegner designed the octagonal structure. The talents of François-Joseph Graf and Pierre Bergé were put to good use in decorating the reception area.

Right. Here, at the home of the director of the Yves Saint Laurent Foundation. we find an exceptional island of greenery in the middle of Paris' 7th arrondissement. A canopy and gravel walkway connects the two verandas on the property.

Useful Addresses

PATIO AND PORCH CONSTRUCTION

CHRISTY WEBBER LANDSCAPES
(DESIGN & CONSTRUCTION, BRICK/STONE PAVING, GARDEN PONDS, LIGHTING)
www.christywebber.com
P: 312-829-2926

GARDENTILE
(LANDSCAPE ARCHITECTURE DESIGN-BUILD FIRM: STONEWORK, CARPENTRY, HARDSCAPE CONSTRUCTION)
www.gardentile.com
P: 206-285-8503

LAWRENCE DESIGN & LANDSCAPING INC.
(BRICK PATIOS AND WALKWAYS, RAISED PATIOS AND PORCHES)
www.lawrencelandscaping.com
P: 716-289-4814

SCREEN TIGHT
(PORCH-ENCLOSING VINYL SLIDING SCREENS)
www.screentight.com
P: 800-768-7325

SUN BOSS CORPORATION
(PATIO CONSTRUCTION, AWNINGS, WALKWAYS, ELECTRICAL NEEDS)
www.sunboss.com
P: 909-782-2360

OUTDOOR FURNITURE

BARLOW TYRIE
(TEAK GARDEN FURNITURE)
www.barlowtyrie.com
P: 800-451-7467

BROWN JORDAN
(ALUMINUM, STAINLESS STEEL, TEAK CHAIRS AND TABLES, UMBRELLAS, ACCESSORIES)
www.brownjordanfurniture.com
P: 800-743-4252

DELGRECO
(LUXURY OUTDOOR FURNITURE)
www.delgrecoandcompany.com
P: 212-688-5310 (NEW YORK)
P: 954-889-0990 (FLORIDA)

HELTZER
(OUTDOOR METAL, STONE, TEXTILE AND WOOD FURNITURE)
www.heltzer.com
P: 877-561-5612

HENRY HALL
(OUTDOOR TEAK FURNISHINGS)
www.henryhalldesigns.com
P: 800-767-7738

JANUS ET CIE
(INTERNATIONAL OUTDOOR FURNISHINGS AND DESIGN CONSULTING)
www.janusetcie.com
P: 800-24-JANUS

LLYOD FLANDERS
(ALL-WEATHER WICKER AND ALUMINUM FURNITURE)
www.lloydflanders.com
P: 888-227-2852

MAINE COTTAGE
(WICKER FURNITURE)
www.mainecottage.com
P: 207-846-1430

MCGUIRE
(RATTAN, WOVEN
AND TEAK FURNITURE)
www.bakerfurniture.com
P: 800-662-4847

MCKINNON & HARRIS
(WROUGHT
ALUMINUM GARDEN
SEATS, TABLES)
www.mckinnonharris.com
P: 804-358-2385

MICHAEL TAYLOR DESIGNS
(SOLID CAST ALUMINUM,
FAUX-STONE OUTDOOR
FURNITURE)
www.michaeltaylordesigns.com

MODERNICA
(STAINLESS STEEL FURNITURE)
www.modernica.net
P: 323-934-1254

PIER 1 IMPORTS
(GARDEN FURNITURE,
GARDEN DECOR
AND LIGHTING)
www.pier1.com
P: 800-245-4595

RESTORATION HARDWARE
(GARDEN FURNITURE,
GARDEN DECOR AND
LIGHTING)
www.restorationhardware.com
P: 800-762-1005

RICHARD SCHULTZ
(MODERN GARDEN FURNITURE
IN ALUMINUM, STAINLESS
STEEL AND WOOD)
www.richardschultz.com

SUTHERLAND
(CLASSIC TEAK FURNITURE)
www.sutherlandteak.com
P: 800-717-8325

TERENCE CONRAN SHOP
(OUTDOOR FURNISHINGS)
www.conran.com
P: 866-755-9079

TROPITONE
(CAST ALUMINUM AND
EXTRUDED ALUMINUM PATIO
FURNITURE, UMBRELLAS)
www.tropitone.com
P: 800-654-7000

WALTERS WICKER
(WICKER, RATTAN AND
WOVEN PEEL FURNITURE)
www.homeportfolio.com
P: 954-929-3030

WEATHEREND
(HEIRLOOM QUALITY
OUTDOOR FURNITURE,
CUSTOM FURNITURE)
www.weatherend.com
P: 800-456-6483

WICKER WORKS
(WICKER, RATTAN, IRON,
TEAK, CARVED WOOD AND
WOVEN HEMP FURNITURE)
www.thewickerworks.com
P: 415-970-5400

PATIO AND PORCH ACCESSORIES

ABC CARPET & HOME
(CANDLES, VASES,
CUSHION FABRIC AND TRIM)
www.abchome.com
P: 212-473-3000

CHRISTIAN TORTU
(VASES, FLORAL DESIGN)
P: 888-955-7550

CRATE & BARREL
(UMBRELLAS, PLANT STANDS,
HAMMOCKS, CASUAL
FURNITURE)
www.crateandbarrel.com
P: 800-967-6696

MECOX GARDENS
(ANTIQUE GARDEN
ORNAMENTS)
www.mecoxgardens.com
P: 212-249-5301 (NEW YORK)
P: 561-805-8611 (FLORIDA)

POTTERY BARN
(ACCESSORIES)
www.potterybarn.com
P: 888-779-5176

SUNBRELLA
(OUTDOOR FABRIC
FOR AWNINGS AND
CUSHIONS)
www.sunbrella.com
P: 336-221-2211

GARDEN AND NURSERY SUPPLIES

CHELSEA GARDEN CENTER
(PLANTS, POTTERY,
FOUNTAINS, FURNISHINGS)
www.chelseagardencenter.com
P: 877-846-0565

LEXINGTON GARDENS
(GARDEN AND
NURSERY SUPPLIES)
P: 212-861-4390

RECYCLING THE PAST
(GARDEN STATUARY,
PLANTERS, FOUNTAINS)
www.recyclingthepast.com
P: 609-660-9790

SEIBERT & RICE
(ITALIAN TERRA COTTA
PLANTERS, URNS,
ACCESSORIES)
www.seibert-rice.com
P: 973-467-8266

SMITH & HAWKEN
(PLANTS, FLOWERS,
ACCESSORIES,
GARDENING TOOLS)
www.smithandhawken.com
P: 800-940-1170

Photographs:

Roland Beaufre: p. 29.
Fernando Bengoechdea: pp. 68-69.
Guy Bouchet: pp. 32, 43, 82, 83, 107.
Gilles de Chabaneix: pp. 30 (right), 34, 35, 40, 42, 72, 73, 77, 80, 85, 88, 89, 90, 100, 112, 114, 115, 118, 119.
Stephen Clément: p. 61.
Jérôme Darblay: p. 84.
Jacques Dirand: pp. 28, 81, 102, 103.
Alain Gelberger: p. 91.
Marianne Haas: pp. 12, 15, 25, 26, 36-38, 41, 44-51, 53 (right), 56, 57, 60, 62, 64, 65, 66, 74, 76, 78, 79, 92, 96, 97, 104-105, 113.
Guillaume de Laubier: cover, pp. 10, 11, 13, 16, 17, 23, 24, 33, 39, 52, 53 (left), 54-55, 63, 86, 87, 94, 95, 99, 101, 106, 109-111, 116, 117.
André Martin: p. 108.
Nicolas Mathéus: pp. 58-59, 59, 70, 71, 75, 120, 121.
Hugh Palmer/Thames & Hudson: pp. 31, 67.
Patrice Pascal: pp. 18-22, 93.
Tuca Reines: p. 98.
Vincent Thibert: p. 30 (left).
Gilles Trillard: pp. 8, 9, 14, 27.

Words and style:

Alexandra d'Arnoux: pp. 29, 74, 84.
Alexandra d'Arnoux and Marie-Claude Dumoulin: pp. 89, 115.
François Baudot: pp. 17, 37, 41, 60, 92.
Marie-Claire Blanckaert: pp. 8-16, 23-27, 31, 33-36, 38, 52-57, 64-67, 76, 78, 79, 86, 87, 94-97, 99, 101, 104-105, 106, 108-111, 113, 116, 117.
Barbara Bourgois: pp. 18-22, 32, 107, 112.
Mario de Castro: p. 98.
Catherine de Chabaneix: pp. 42, 114.
Françoise Delbecq: p. 62
Francis Dorléans: pp. 68-69.
Laurence Dougier: pp. 58-59, 59, 70, 71, 75, 120, 121.
Marie-Claude Dumoulin: p. 30 (right).
Marie-Claude Dumoulin and Barbara Bourgois, assisted by Andréa Lucas-Pauwels: pp. 102, 103.
Niccolo Grassi: pp. 44-51.
Marie Kalt: pp. 28, 40, 43, 63, 82, 83, 88, 90.
Françoise Labro: p. 81.
Andréa Lucas-Pauwels: p. 91.
Misha de Potestad: p. 39.
Isabelle Rosanis: p. 61.
Catherine Scotto: pp. 30 (left), 93.
Paul-Marie Sorel: pp. 72, 118.
Francine Vormèse: pp. 73, 77, 80, 85, 100, 119.

Elle Decor (U.S.) and *Elle Décoration* (France) are both imprints of the Hachette Filipacchi group.
The content of this book was taken solely from *Elle Décoration* and appeared only in France.

WE WOULD LIKE TO THANK THE OWNERS, DECORATORS, ARCHITECTS, INSTITUTIONS AND HOTELS THAT WELCOMED *ELLE DECOR* COLLABORATORS FOR THIS PUBLICATION:

GERARD AMSALLEM, GUY ANDRE, CHRISTIAN BADIN, KEVIN BAKER, LOUIS BENECH, PIERRE BERGE, JEAN-MICHEL BEURDELEY, DIDIER BOEGNER, FABIENNE BOUDET, LAURENT BOURGOIS, MURIEL BRANDOLINI, GUY BRETON, BOGDAN BRZECZKOWSKI, LAURENCE AND PHILIPPE BRUNON, PASTRI BUNNAG, PASCAL CRIBIER, GEORGES DAMBIER, PHILIPPE DAREL, MR. DELAFAILLE, ALAIN DEMACHY (GALERIE CAMOIN), JULIA ERRERA, AHMET AND MICA ERTEGUN, TONY FACELLA, PATRICK FRÈCHE, JOHN FRIEDA, ANNE-MARIE DE GANAY, JEAN-MICHEL GATHY, ANNICK GOUTAL, FRANÇOIS-JOSEPH GRAF, COUNT DE GRIVEL, JACQUELINE HAGNAUER, ANOUSKA HEMPEL, VIOLETT AND JEAN HENSON, TERRY HUNZIKER, ALAIN DAVID IDOUX, MICHELLE JOUBERT, DOMINIQUE KIEFFER, PIERRE LACOMBE, JACQUES MAJORELLE, ANGELA MASSI, MED, TEDDY MILLINGTON-DRAKE, NICOLE MUGLER, ALAIN-DOMINIQUE PERRIN, MARIE-JOSE POMMEREAU, JULIE PRISCA, GIOVANNA RAINIERI, OLIVIER RIOLS, PIERRE ALEXANDRE RISSER, JEAN-MARC ROQUES, LARY ROSENBERG, THE ROTHSCHILD FAMILY, YVES SAINT LAURENT, CHIRA SHILPAKANOK, SHARON SIMONAIRE, PHILIPPE STARCK, JOHN STEFANIDIS, YVES TARALON, ED TUTTLE, VALENTINO, GIANNI VERSACE, AMÉLIE VIGNERAS, GORDON WATSON, JACQUES WIRTZ; THE CITY OF MARSEILLE, THE GEA, THE MAISON-MUSEE EUREKA, THE FREDERICO DE FREITAS MUSEUM, THE HOTELS AMANPURI, AMANWANA, CHAUFOURG AND COTTON HOUSE.

**Under the direction of
Jean Demachy**

Editorial
Sophie Lilienfeld

Art Direction
Marie-France Fèvre-Couanault